COLONIAL

CLOTHES

Verna Fisher

COLONIAL
QUEST

Nomad Press
A division of Nomad Communications
10 9 8 7 6 5 4 3 2 1

This book was manufactured by
Regal Printing Limited in China
June 2010, Job #1005018
ISBN: 978-1-936313-04-4

Illustrations by Andrew Christensen

Questions regarding the ordering of this book should be addressed to
Independent Publishers Group
814 N. Franklin St.
Chicago, IL 60610
www.ipgbook.com

Nomad Press
2456 Christian St.
White River Junction, VT 05001
www.nomadpress.net

3|23

Contents

MAP ~ TIMELINE

chapter 1
WHAT COLONIAL PEOPLE WORE~page 1

chapter 2
SPINNING THREAD AND WEAVING CLOTH~page 5

chapter 3
COBBLERS AND TANNERS~page 11

chapter 4
MILLINERS AND WIGMAKERS~page 15

chapter 5
NATIVE AMERICAN CLOTHING~page 19

Glossary ~ Further Investigations ~ Index

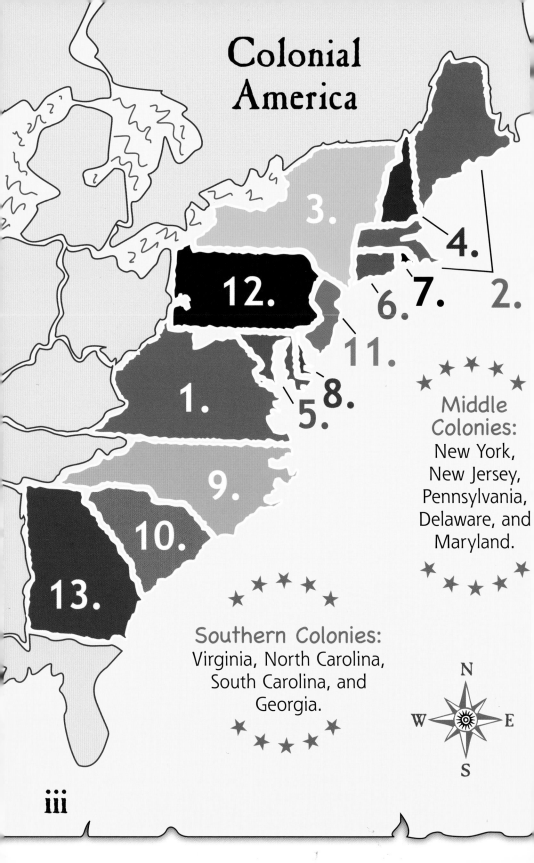

Colonial America

3.

4.

2.

12.

6. 7.

11.

1.

5. 8.

9.

10.

13.

Middle
Colonies:
New York,
New Jersey,
Pennsylvania,
Delaware, and
Maryland.

Southern Colonies:
Virginia, North Carolina,
South Carolina, and
Georgia.

N
W ✦ E
S

New England:
Massachusetts,
New Hampshire, Connecticut,
and Rhode Island.

In the 1600s, people began leaving Europe to settle in America. Some were explorers searching for gold, while others came looking for freedom.

Jamestown in Virginia and Plymouth in Massachusetts were two of the earliest settlements where these people came to start a new life.

1. Virginia

2. Massachusetts

3. New York

4. New Hampshire

5. Maryland

6. Connecticut

7. Rhode Island

8. Delaware

9. North Carolina

10. South Carolina

11. New Jersey

12. Pennsylvania

13. Georgia

What Colonial People Wore

When the colonists first settled in the New World, there were no stores selling clothes. Of course, the colonists brought clothes with them from England.

Words to Know

Colonial adults and children dressed pretty much the same way. Children looked like small grown-ups.

But what happened when these clothes wore out or children outgrew them? The colonists either had to make their own or order more from supply ships.

colonist: a person who came to settle America.

New World: what is now America. It was called the New World by people from Europe because it was new to them.

Then and Now

In colonial times shoes had buckles.

Today your shoes have laces or Velcro.

Men and boys in Colonial America wore breeches with long white stockings that came up to their knees. They also wore white shirts and vests, with long coats over the vests.

Colonial women and girls wore floor-length dresses. They often wore an apron over the dress, and a bonnet on their head.

Colonial America: the name given to America when talking about the years 1607–1776.

breeches: tight-fitting pants that go to the knees.

bonnet: a hat made out of cloth or straw, tied with ribbons.

Did You Know?

Hoop skirts made it hard to sit down. If a woman didn't sit down in just the right way, her hoop skirt would FLY UP in front of her face. That must have been embarrassing!

Gowns with hoop skirts underneath were popular among wealthy women. Hoop skirts made the gowns look rounded and puffy.

Words to Know

4

Spinning Thread and Weaving Cloth

Clothes from England were expensive and took a long time to arrive in the colonies by ship. For this reason, many colonial women made clothes for their families.

colonies: early settlements in America.

fibers: fine short threads. Fibers twisted together make long strands of yarn and thread.

Words to Know

Making fabric and sewing it into clothing was a big job. All the girls in the family helped. First they had to make thread, then weave the thread into fabric.

Thread was made from cotton or wool **fibers.** Cotton grows on the cotton plant. Wool comes from the coat of sheep.

Women used spinning wheels to twist fibers into thread. Pressing on the foot pedal turned the wheel.

The spinning wheel pulls on the fibers and twists them into thread.

6

After the thread was washed and dyed, colonial women used weaving looms to weave the thread into fabric. Then the fabric was cut and sewed into clothes.

Words to Know

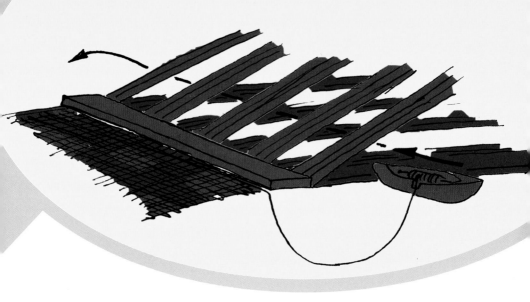

The colonists weren't allowed to weave their own fabrics or even own sheep. Why? The King of England wanted the colonists to buy their cloth from England.

Many colonists felt that this was unfair. They went against the law by owning sheep and making cloth.

dye: to make a color.

loom: a large machine used to weave thread into fabric.

Then and Now

In colonial times the women and girls made clothes for the entire family.

Today your family buys clothes from a store.

Eventually, **weavers** came to the New World and set up weaving shops. **Tailors** came to the colonies to sew clothes for men and women. Gown-makers sewed dresses for women.

Breeches, gowns, and coats were **custom made** for everyone, including slaves. The difference between clothing for the wealthy, the poor, and slaves was in how fine the fabric was.

Words to Know

weaver: a person who uses a loom to make cloth.

tailor: a person who makes and repairs clothing.

custom made: made just for you.

Cobblers and Tanners

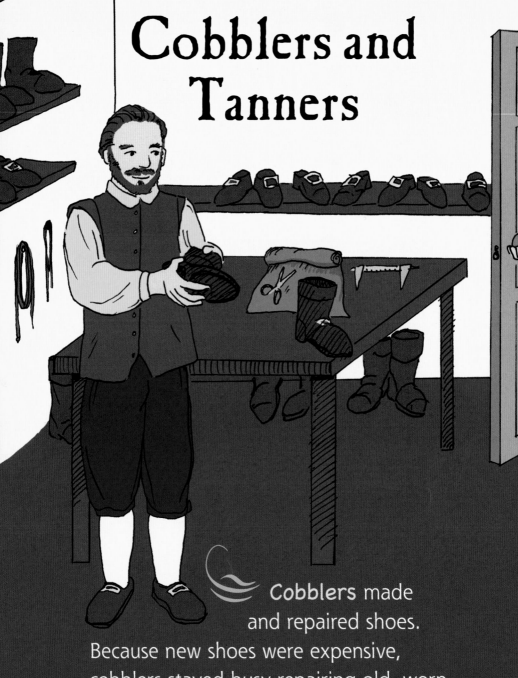

Cobblers made and repaired shoes. Because new shoes were expensive, cobblers stayed busy repairing old, worn-out shoes. Most shoes were made from leather.

The colonists used leather for shoes, belts, bags, and saddles.

cobbler: a person who makes and repairs shoes.

leather: the tanned skin of an animal.

Words to Know

Did You Know?

Shoes could be worn on either foot.
No worrying about lefts and rights!

Tanners turned animal skins into leather. Tanning was a long process that involved scraping, soaking, and washing the skins many times.

★ Then and Now

In colonial times shoes were heavy and clumsy to wear.

Today you wear comfortable sneakers.

Words to Know

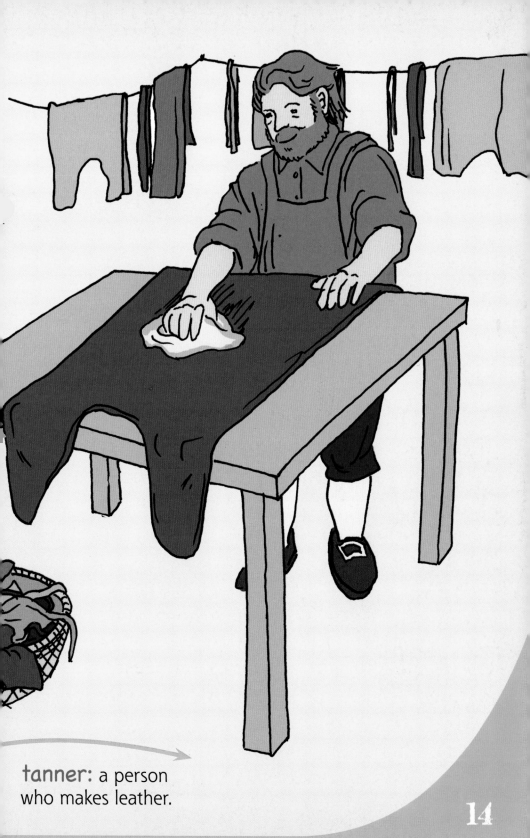

tanner: a person
who makes leather.

14

Milliners and Wigmakers

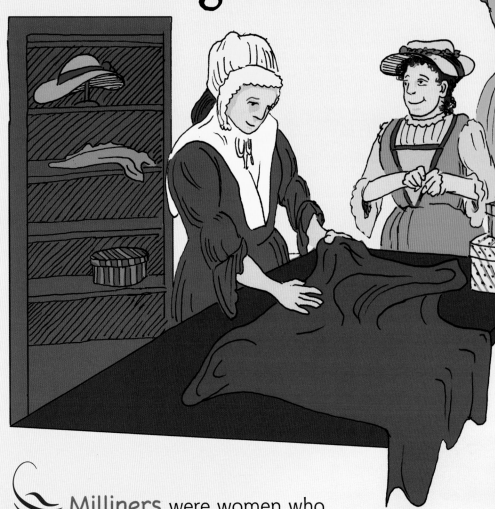

Milliners were women who owned shops that sold fabric. They also sold fashion items imported from Europe, such as gloves, hats, shoes, and jewelry.

Words to Know

milliner: a person who sells fabric, hats, and other fashion accessories.

cloak: a coat worn over the shoulders like a cape.

muff: a fur sleeve, with two open ends.

Milliners mended clothing and made **cloaks** and **muffs**. On cold days, colonial women put their hands into a muff to stay warm.

Wigmakers made wigs out of horse, goat, yak, or human hair. Wigs became popular after King Louis XIII of France started wearing one because he was losing his hair.

Many men and women wore wigs even if they had hair, trying to be in style. Some wealthy landowners even had their slaves wear wigs for important occasions.

Did You Know?

In colonial times people put powder and perfume onto their wigs to make them smell better!

17

Then and Now

In colonial times people copied kings and wore wigs to be in style.

Today people copy the way movie stars and famous athletes dress.

Wigs were very expensive. The wigmaker sewed curled hair into a cap. Wigs were custom made to fit the customer's head.

Customers could choose from many different styles. The most formal wigs had white hair, with a ribbon tied around a ponytail or braid in the back.

18

Native American Clothing

Native Americans were the people who already lived in America when the colonists arrived. They made their clothing from the skins of animals they hunted and trapped. Leather was used to make bags, clothing, and shoes.

Words to Know

wampum: Native American necklaces, belts, and bracelets made from shells.

The Native Americans made beads, belts, necklaces, and bracelets out of shells, called wampum. The shells were mostly white, with purple used to create designs. When the colonists began trading with the Native Americans, wampum became a form of money.

Different groups of Native Americans wore different styles of clothing. Most men wore breechcloths, with leather leggings if it was cold. In some groups, men wore kilts or fur trousers instead of breechcloths.

Some Native American women wore skirts and leggings. Others wore dresses.

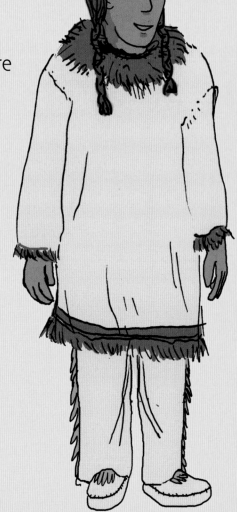

Nearly all Native Americans wore some form of moccasin. Fur cloaks, which were animal skins with the fur left on, made good winter clothing.

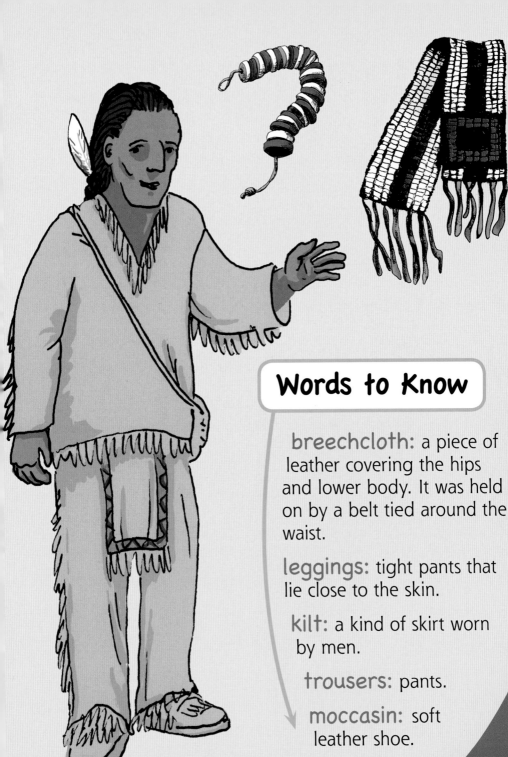

Words to Know

breechcloth: a piece of leather covering the hips and lower body. It was held on by a belt tied around the waist.

leggings: tight pants that lie close to the skin.

kilt: a kind of skirt worn by men.

trousers: pants.

moccasin: soft leather shoe.

The Native Americans used the claws and teeth of animals for jewelry and to decorate clothing.

Then and Now

In colonial times people wore clothing made from cotton, wool, and animal skins. These are natural materials.

Today you might still wear clothing made from leather, cotton, and wool. But you also wear clothing made from new materials that are manmade, such as polyester.

After the colonists came to the New World, Native American clothing started to change. As the colonists took up more and more land, native groups started to live closer to each other. They borrowed from each other's styles of clothing. Native Americans also added pieces of European clothing to their outfits.

Glossary

bonnet: a hat made out of cloth or straw, tied with ribbons.

breechcloth: a piece of leather covering the hips and lower body, held on by a belt tied around the waist.

breeches: tight-fitting pants that go to the knees.

cloak: a coat worn over the shoulders like a cape.

cobbler: a person who makes and repairs shoes.

Colonial America: the name given to America when talking about the years 1607–1776.

colonies: early settlements in America.

colonist: a person who came to settle America.

custom made: made just for you.

dye: to make a color.

fibers: fine short threads. When twisted together fibers make long strands of yarn and thread.

hoop skirt: a garment worn under a gown to make it puff out.

kilt: a kind of skirt worn by men.

leather: the tanned skin of an animal.

leggings: tight pants that lie close to the skin.

loom: a large machine used to weave thread into fabric.

milliner: a person who sells fabric, hats, and other fashion accessories.

moccasin: soft leather shoe.

muff: a fur sleeve, with two open ends.

New World: what is now America. It was called the New World by people from Europe because it was new to them.

spinning wheel: a tool used to make thread or yarn out of cotton or wool.

tailor: a person who makes and repairs clothing.

tanner: a person who makes leather.

trousers: pants.

wampum: Native American necklaces, belts, and bracelets made from shells.

weaver: a person who uses a loom to make cloth.

Further Investigations

Books

Bordessa, Kris. *Great Colonial America Projects You Can Build Yourself.* White River Junction, VT: Nomad Press, 2006.

Fisher, Verna. *Explore Colonial America! 25 Great Projects, Activities, Experiments.* White River Junction, VT: Nomad Press, 2009.

Museums and Websites

Colonial Williamsburg
www.history.org
Williamsburg, Virginia

National Museum of the American Indian
www.nmai.si.edu
Washington, D.C. and New York, New York

Plimoth Plantation
www.plimoth.org
Plymouth, Massachusetts

America's Library
www.americaslibrary.gov

Jamestown Settlement
www.historyisfun.org

Native American History
www.bigorrin.org

Native Languages of the Americas
www.native-languages.org

Social Studies for Kids
www.socialstudiesforkids.com

The Mayflower
www.mayflowerhistory.com

Virtual Jamestown
www.virtualjamestown.org

Index

B
bags, 12, 19
belts, 12, 20
breechcloths, 21

C
children, 2
cloaks, 16, 21
cobblers, 11–12
cotton, 6, 24

D
dresses/skirts, 3–4, 9, 21

F
fabric, 6–9, 15
fur, 16, 17, 21

G
gloves, 15

H
hats/bonnets, 3, 15
hoop skirts, 4

J
Jamestown, Virginia, iv
jewelry, 15, 20, 23

L
leather, 11–13, 19, 21, 24
leggings, 21

M
map of colonies, iii
men/boys' clothing, 3, 21
milliners, 15–16
moccasins, 21
muffs, 16

N
Native American clothing,
    19–24

P
pants/breeches/trousers,
    3, 21
Plymouth,
    Massachusetts, iv

S
sewing, 6, 9, 16
sheep, 6, 8
shells, 20
shoes, 3, 11, 13, 15,
    19, 21
slaves, 9, 17
spinning wheels, 6

T
tailors, 9
tanners, 13–14
thread, 6–7
timeline, iv

W
wampum, 20
weavers/weaving, 6–9
wigs/wigmakers, 17–18
women/girls, 3–10,
    16, 21
wool, 6, 8, 24